# Get Growing!
## Exciting Indoor Plant Projects for Kids

### Lois Walker

John Wiley & Sons, Inc.
New York • Chichester • Brisbane • Toronto • Singapore

**Library of Congress Cataloging-in-Publication Data**

Walker, Lois, 1941–
   Get growing! : exciting indoor plant projects for kids / by Lois Walker.
      p.   cm.
   Summary: Presents eleven indoor gardening projects involving carrots, beans, potatoes, apples, and other plants, and related cooking and handicraft activities.
   ISBN 0-471-54488-4
   1. Vegetable gardening—Juvenile literature.   2. Indoor gardening—Juvenile literature.   3. Fruit-culture—Juvenile literature.
   4. Cookery (Vegetables)—Juvenile literature.   5. Cookery (Fruit)—Juvenile literature.   6. Handicraft—Juvenile literature.
   [1. Indoor gardening.   2. Cookery—Vegetables.   3. Handicraft.]
   I. Title.
   SB324.5.W35   1991
   635—dc20
                                                                91-13412
                                                                     AC

Printed in the United States of America

10   9   8   7   6   5   4   3   2   1

# CONTENTS

# INTRODUCTION

You don't need a green thumb to grow beautiful indoor plants. All you need are a few basic instructions, some special food items from the kitchen, and an interest in growing things.

*Get Growing!* describes eleven exciting plant projects — from easy-to-grow greenery for beginners to a more challenging final project for the more experienced young gardener.

And yes, it's true, you can grow most of these plants from food in your own kitchen. Carrots, potatoes, popping corn, peanuts (in shells), and seeds from certain fresh fruit can all be turned into potted plants. And by following the easy, step-by-step directions in the book you can make crafts to go with your plants and tasty treats to eat from plant "leftovers."

Most of the projects can be done with little help from grown-ups, so roll up your sleeves, activate your thumb, whether it's green or not, and *get growing*!

# HELPFUL HINTS

### Get it together

Once you've decided on a project, check the materials to make sure you have everything you need. Don't start until everything is in its place.

### Organize

Cover your work area with old newspapers or a plastic tablecloth. Arrange all tools and materials on the work area in front of you. Sometimes a basement, garage, porch, workshop, or outside area is best for messy plant projects.

### Add some common sense

Ask an adult to help with sharp tools, fire and heat, chemicals, or tricky instructions.

### Clean up and smile

When you've completed your project, please sweep up spilled soil, throw scraps out, wash utensils, and put everything away. Don't forget to smile!

# IMPORTANT WORDS

Knowing the meanings of these important words or phrases will help you with your plant projects. If you forget a meaning, don't worry. Just check back to this page.

**Dust**    Covering a plant's leaves with a light coat of protective powder. You can *dust* a plant just as you might dust yourself with after-bath powder.

**Feed**    Giving fertilizer or plant food to your plants. Always read directions on the package so you can feed your plants properly.

**Mist**    Spraying a fine *mist* of water on plants, soil, or inside your glass-jar greenhouse.

**Plant**    Placing a seed or seedling in soil so that it will take root and grow.

**Soil Mixture**    A basic mix of soil, sand, and peat moss which should work well for all the projects in this book. Use a large bowl or pail and your hands to mix:
   2 parts garden soil
   1 part sand
   1 part peat moss.

**Spiral**    A curve that keeps winding 'round and 'round.

**Sprout**    Placing seeds in an environment which will make them begin to grow.

**Stake and Tie**    Placing a stick or stake firmly in flowerpot soil beside a plant. Gently tie plant's stem to the stake with string. This helps the plant stand up straight and grow upward.

**Tend**    Taking care of your plants by checking them regularly, watering them when they are dry, and making sure they have the kind of sunlight or temperature they need.

**Transplant**    Taking a plant from one place and planting it in another place.

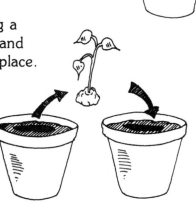

# Carrot Plants

**Potted plant**
**Hanging basket**
**Hot and spicy carrot bread recipe**

# Potted Plant

Here's an easy and inexpensive way to grow your own plant. Did you know that the orange part of a carrot (the root) can provide food for your new greenery — and for you too?

**You will need:**    carrot with leaves        handful of small stones
paring knife                water
low shallow bowl        a sunny place

**1.** Using the knife, cut the leaves off your carrot.

**2.** Cut off *bottom* part of carrot. Wash and eat it, or save it for the recipe on page 15.

**3.** Put the top part of your cut carrot in a shallow dish and put stones all around it.

**4.** Keep water in the dish. Add water when the water in the dish sinks below the top layer of stones.

**5.** Put the dish in a sunny place and check it every day.

**6.** The plant will use the food in its orange root to send up beautiful new leaves.

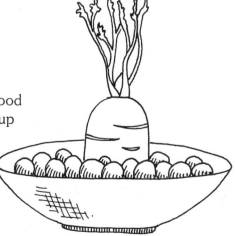

# Hanging Basket

This crazy mixed-up carrot hangs upside down and grows into a miniature hanging plant. Try it in a sunny bathroom or kitchen window where you can water it every day.

**You will need:**
a fat carrot with leaves
paring knife
two strong toothpicks

string
water
a sunny window

**1.** Cut the leaves off your carrot with the paring knife.

**2.** Cut off bottom part of carrot, leaving a nice plump orange section which is about 1 inch (2.5 cm) long.

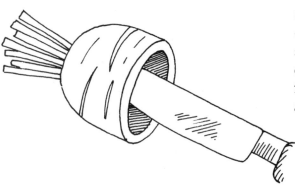

**3.** Turn carrot upside down and use your knife to carve out the centre of the orange section. This hole becomes a carrot watering cup. Be careful with the knife. Ask an adult for help, if needed.

**4.** Stick toothpicks into sides of your cup as shown.

**5.** Now, tie strings to the ends of your toothpicks to make a hanging basket.

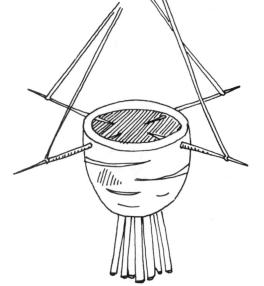

**6.** Hang your unique basket in a sunny window and keep your carrot cup filled with water.

**7.** Who needs a fancy hanging fern? Your carrot will soon grow new leaves and become a showpiece. Believe it or not!

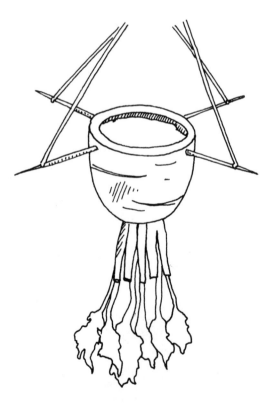

14

# Hot and Spicy Carrot Bread Recipe

The best part about growing new plants from carrots is that you can eat the leftovers! Try this tasty carrot bread and serve it tonight. While you are eating, think about the orange roots which are providing food for both you and your plant to grow on.

**You will need:**

large bowl
electric mixer
flour sifter
large spoon
grater
nut chopper or
   rolling pin and
   two sheets of
   waxed paper
measuring cup
measuring spoons
greased loaf pan
oven

**Ingredients:**

2/3 cup (150 mL) salad oil
1 cup (250 mL) sugar
2 eggs
1-1/2 cups (375 mL) flour
   (white or whole wheat)
1 teaspoon (5 mL) baking
   soda
1 teaspoon (5 mL) cinnamon
1 teaspoon (5 mL) nutmeg
1/2 teaspoon (2 mL) salt
1 cup (250 mL) grated carrot
1/2 cup (125 mL) chopped
   nuts
3/4 cup (175 mL) raisins

**1.** Put 2/3 cup (150 mL) salad oil and 1 cup (250 mL) sugar in bowl. Mix with electric mixer until creamy.

**2.** Add 2 eggs to bowl. Stir.

**3.** Put 1-1/2 cups (375 mL) flour, 1 teaspoon (5 mL) baking soda, 1 teaspoon (5 mL) cinnamon, 1 teaspoon (5 mL) nutmeg, and 1/2 teaspoon (2 mL) salt into sifter. Sift all into the egg mixture. Stir.

**4.** Add 1 cup (250 mL) grated carrots and 3/4 cup (175 mL) raisins. Stir.

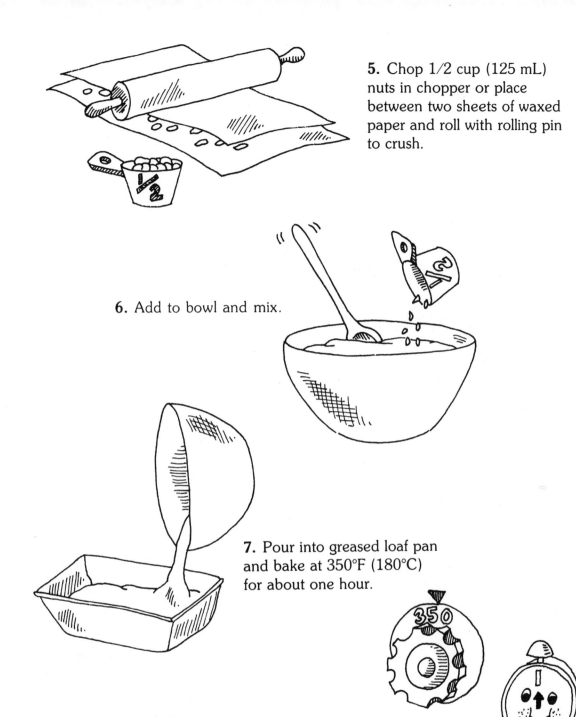

**5.** Chop 1/2 cup (125 mL) nuts in chopper or place between two sheets of waxed paper and roll with rolling pin to crush.

**6.** Add to bowl and mix.

**7.** Pour into greased loaf pan and bake at 350°F (180°C) for about one hour.

**A Special Gift:**

Give a carrot plant, a loaf of carrot bread, and the recipe to a favorite friend. The plant will be a cheerful reminder of your friendship long after the bread is gone.

# Citrus Seed Plants

**Planting a citrus seed**
**Gift ideas**

# Planting a Citrus Seed

Citrus fruit is a healthy and delicious treat, but don't eat the seeds. Save them for planting and you'll soon have a houseplant with dark shiny leaves.

**You will need:**

clay pot, plastic
   container,
   or paper cup
saucer
small stones
garden soil

sand
bowl for mixing
peat moss
your fattest citrus seeds
water
a sunny window

**1.** Save the fattest lemon, orange, or grapefruit seeds and let them dry out in the air for one week. Remember, cooked seeds won't grow.

**2.** If your planting pot has no hole in the bottom, make one now. A pencil makes a good hole in the bottom of a paper cup. Ask an adult to help you make a hole in a plastic container, using a sharp knife or heated nail.

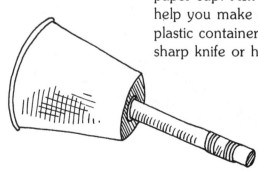

**3.** Put a few small stones in the planting pot and cover the hole.

**4.** Time to mix the soil. Ask an adult to help with measuring, if needed. Use a bowl and your hands to mix:
   2 parts garden soil
   1 part sand
   1 part peat moss.

**5.** Fill planting pot almost to the top with soil mixture. Make a small hole in the soil with your finger.

**6.** Now, put your dried seed in the hole and cover it with soil. Make new holes and plant more seeds if you want, but put all orange seeds in **one** pot. Put lemon seeds in another. Put grapefruit seeds in another.

**7.** Label the pots so you'll know what kind of seeds are planted in each pot. Put on saucers and place in a sunny window.

**8.** Water your seeds every day, but give them just a little water. Soil should stay moist, but not really wet. Some people squeeze a wet sponge over their seeds to water them.

**9.** When one plant grows big and strong, remove other plants and let the strongest one have the pot to itself.

**10.** As your plant grows even bigger, you will have to transplant it into a bigger pot.

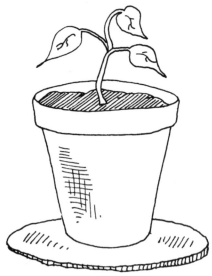

It's a miracle! A shiny new houseplant grows from a tiny seed — with just a little help from you.

# Gift Ideas

If you plan to give one of your seed plants to someone as a gift, decorate the planting pot with pictures of lemons, oranges, or grapefruit. Attach a home-made card. You might print this poem on the front of your card:

Hi there, I'm a _____ plant.
Some people say I can grow a _____
And some people say I can't.

I'll work on that when I get bigger
But now, to keep me going
I need moist soil, a sunny home
And your love — to keep me growing.

Look inside for a special way
To use my juicy fruit someday.

# "Hi there, I'm a <u>LEMON</u> plant!"

**Print these directions inside** *lemon* **card:**

Invisible writing! You can send an invisible message to a friend and *only* your friend will know the decoding secret.

**1.** Squeeze the juice from a lemon into a small bowl.

**2.** Now, dip a thin brush or clean pen into the juice.

**3.** Using the juice as ink, write or paint a secret message on a piece of paper.

**4.** When the juice dries, it will not show and will seem invisible.

**5.** Decoding Secret: The message will become visible when your friend holds the paper over a bare lightbulb.

"Hi there, I'm an ORANGE plant!"

**Print these directions inside *orange* card:**

Dried orange peel spirals are pretty to look at and smell so good. Keep them in the house and they become natural air fresheners.

1. Using knife, cut skin off orange in one long strip. Start at top of orange and work around and around until you get to the bottom. Be careful with the knife. Ask an adult for help, if needed.

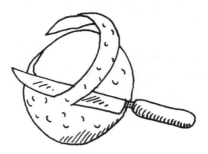

2. With your fingers, curl the strip into a tight spiral. Some people like to curl their strips into rosette shapes.

3. Dry your spirals in a warm, dry place. Avoid moisture. Spirals will become hard and dry in about one week.

4. Arrange your spirals in a basket with dried flowers or leaves. Every time you enjoy the fragrance, please think of me.

# "Hi there, I'm a GRAPEFRUIT plant!"

**Print these directions inside**
*grapefruit* **card:**

Hot granola grapefruit. Hope
you will enjoy this speedy
and delicious breakfast idea.

**1.** Cut grapefruit in half and
remove seeds. Remove core,
if you wish.

**2.** Loosen all small grapefruit
sections on three sides, but
leave them in their spaces.

**3.** Mix 1/2 cup (125 mL)
granola and 2 tablespoons
(25 mL) honey. Spread this
mixture over each half.

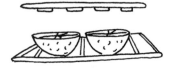

**4.** Put the two sections on a
metal tray and place under
oven broiler and broil until it
bubbles or microwave on
high for 2 or 3 minutes. Ask
an adult for help with the
broiler setting, if needed.

# Bean Plants

**Sprouting a bean in a drinking glass**
**Bean-in-a-cup**
**"Oats, Peas, Beans, and Barley Grow" song**

# Sprouting a Bean in a Drinking Glass

*"Do you or I or anyone know how oats, peas, beans, and barley grow?"* Plant a bean in your drinking glass and watch it carefully. Soon you'll know exactly what happens to a bean when you plant it, like a farmer does, in the earth.

**You will need:**

a drinking glass you
    can see through
blotter paper (from
    office supply store)
    or a paper towel
scissors

cotton
seed beans (cooked
    beans will not grow)
water
a sunny window

**1.** With your scissors, cut a strip of blotter paper (or paper towel) long enough to go around the outside of your drinking glass. The strip should be 2 or 3 inches (5 to 7 cm) wide.

**2.** Now, put your strip all around the *inside* of your glass. Leave it there.

**3.** Fill the drinking glass with cotton or cotton balls.

**4.** Slowly pour water over the cotton so that the cotton becomes *damp* but not *wet*. It is too wet if you can see water standing in the bottom of the glass.

**5.** Place some bean seeds inside the drinking glass between the paper and the glass. You should be able to see the beans clearly.

**6.** Put the glass close to a sunny window and keep the cotton DAMP.

**7.** As the seeds soak up water, they will get fatter and fatter until — their skins pop!

**8.** You'll soon see your seed beans changing. A tiny plant lives inside the bean and gets its food from the bean.

**9.** If you watch carefully, you'll finally see the small leaves of that tiny plant. Let them grow.

**10.** Transplant your bean plant into a pot or container almost filled with soil mixture. Place the pot on a saucer.

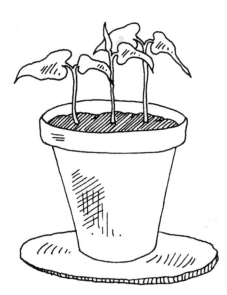

**11.** When the leaves of your plant turn green, you'll know that the plant can finally make its own food.

# How a bean grows:

If you watch carefully, you will see your beans grow like this:

Later, your bean plant makes its food from soil, sun, and water:

# Bean-in-a-Cup

You can also sprout a bean using only some yarn, water, and a paper cup.

**1.** Arrange thick yarn in a spiral pattern in the bottom of a paper cup. Completely fill bottom of cup with spiral.

**2.** Add water to cup so that yarn is *damp*. No water should stand in cup above the yarn.

**3.** Carefully drop a few seed beans on to the yarn.

**4.** Place in sunny spot and keep yarn *moist*.

**5.** When your seed beans develop roots, plant them outside or in a soil-filled flowerpot.

*Clap your hands to the rhythm and recite the words below. Try this as a circle game with a "farmer" in the centre who acts out the movements. Your family and friends can join hands to make the circle. Change "farmers" on every verse. Can you imagine the beans growing?*

**Key of E♭**

Oats, Peas, Beans, and Bar – ley Grow

*First, the farmer sows his seed,*
*Stands erect and takes his ease.*
*He stamps his foot and claps his hands*
*And turns around to view his lands.*

Chorus:
*Oats, peas, beans, and barley grow.*
*Oats, peas, beans, and barley grow.*
*Can you or I or anyone know*
*How oats, peas, beans, and barley grow?*

*Next, the farmer waters the seed,*
*Stands erect and takes his ease.*
*He stamps his foot and claps his hands*
*And turns around to view his lands.*

Repeat chorus

*Next, the farmer hoes the weeds,*
*Stands erect and takes his ease.*
*He stamps his foot and claps his hands*
*And turns around to view his lands.*

Repeat chorus

*Last, the farmer harvests his seed,*
*Stands erect and takes his ease.*
*He stamps his foot and claps his hands*
*And turns around to view his lands.*

Repeat chorus

# Potato Plants

**Sweet potato vine**
**White potato potted plant**
**Homemade plant person**

# Sweet Potato Vine

Do you have one potato, two potato, three potato, four? Try cooking three and use the fourth to grow an impressive vine or beautiful potted plant.

**You will need:**   one fat sweet potato       four toothpicks
a drinking glass, small     water
glass vase or glass       a cool dark place
custard cup           a sunny window

1. Find a nice fat sweet potato which easily fits into your glass container or vase.

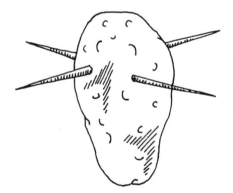

2. Stick four toothpicks into the sides of the sweet potato. Place them all the way around the potato and about half way up.

3. Place the wide end of your sweet potato into the container and rest the toothpicks on the rim of the container. The toothpicks will hold the top of your potato out of the water.

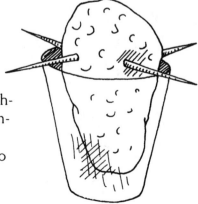

**4.** Now, add water to your container until the bottom of the potato is covered.

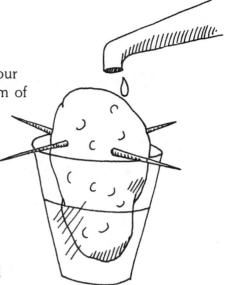

**5.** Put the container and potato in a cool dark place and leave there for one to two weeks.

**6.** When roots grow from the bottom of the potato and stems sprout from the top, place your container near a sunny window.

**7.** Before you know it, you'll see long vines and pretty leaves growing right out of your sweet potato!

# White Potato Potted Plant

What has eyes but cannot see? Potatoes! Many people don't know that you can grow a plant from a white potato. If you plant a potato "eye" with a chunk of its white tuber, the eye will actually grow into a plant. Try it yourself.

**You will need:**
one white potato
paring knife
paper cup
soil mixture

saucer
small stones or pebbles
water
sunny spot

**1.** Keep your white potato in a warm dark place until the eyes start to grow. (The cupboard under the sink is usually a good place.) *Or* find a potato whose eyes are already starting to grow.

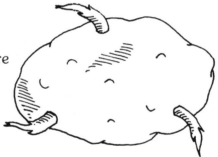

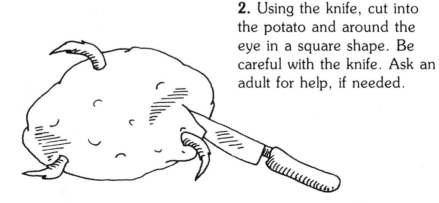

**2.** Using the knife, cut into the potato and around the eye in a square shape. Be careful with the knife. Ask an adult for help, if needed.

**3.** Be sure to cut deep into the potato. Now, cut out a large piece of the potato including the *eye*. Remember that this white chunk of potato is the *food* which the eye will use to start growing.

**4.** Use a pencil to punch a hole in the bottom of your paper cup and fill bottom with pebbles or small stones.

**5.** Almost fill the cup with soil mixture.

**6.** Finally, plant your chunk of potato in the soil. The growing eye should stick out of the soil at the top.

**7.** Put the pot on a saucer. Then water the soil and keep in a sunny spot. How long do you think it will be before you have a new green houseplant?

# Homemade Plant Person

If you don't always have time to talk to your plants, try making a *plant person* who will do it for you. Stick a homemade plant person into the pot with your plant, and they'll both be company for each other.

**You will need:**
old nylon stocking or pantyhose
round cereal bowl
marking pencil
scissors
needle, threaded with knotted thread

cotton balls (or cotton batten)
popsicle stick or small stick from outdoors
glue
assorted decorations

**1.** Using scissors, cut stocking or pantyhose all the way up one side. Open fabric and lay it flat.

**2.** Place bowl (upside down) on stocking and trace around it with marking pencil.

**3.** Remove bowl and cut out circle with scissors.

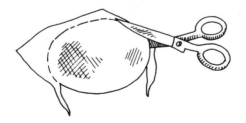

**4.** Using needle and thread, sew large stitches around nylon circle and just inside the edge of that circle.

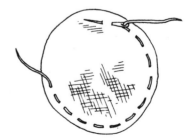

**5.** When you have sewn around to where you started, cut needle off thread but leave thread loose. Don't tie it yet.

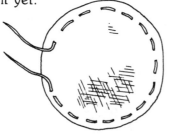

**6.** Place a few cotton balls in the centre of your nylon circle. Now, gently pull end of loose thread and a nylon pouch will begin to form. Keep stuffing cotton inside pouch and adjusting with thread until "head" is the size you like. Remember, you can cover the back of the head with hair so that side need not be perfect.

**7.** When you are satisfied with the head size and shape, tie off the thread.

**8.** Glue stick to head as shown. (If using popsicle sticks, glue two or three sticks together to get the length you need.)

**9.** Now the fun! Using glue, decorate your plant person any way you'd like. You can glue on yarn, feathers, or fur for hair. Try buttons, dried beans or pasta for eyes. Bows, lace, or jewelry can be used for trim. Use your imagination and enjoy yourself.

**10.** When your plant person is finished, stick him or her into the soil around your plant — and make the introductions. We hope they live happily ever after!

*Variation:* Using a needle and thread, sew back and forth through stocking and cotton. Pull thread tight to form protruding nose, lips, eyes, or eyebrows.

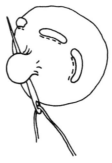

# Pineapple Plants

**Sprouting and potting a pineapple**
**Apple-pineapple surprise**
**Pineapple pine cone partners**
**Pineapple yogurt dip recipe**

# Sprouting and Potting a Pineapple

Next time you buy a fresh pineapple, save part of it and start a new pineapple houseplant. If you take care of the plant, it may grow *very* large!

**You will need:**
one fresh pineapple
sharp knife
glass pie pan or
   shallow dish
pebbles or small stones
crushed charcoal
water
sunny window ledge

**Later:**

flowerpot
saucer
soil mixture

**Note:** Charcoal helps keep water fresh by absorbing small impurities.

**1.** With the sharp knife, cut the leaves from the top of the pineapple, as shown. Be careful with the knife. Ask an adult to help with the cutting, if needed.

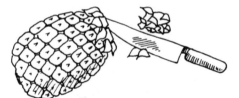

**2.** Slice off pineapple fruit leaving only 2 to 3 inches (5 to 7 cm) of fruit at the top.

**3.** You are going to grow new leaves from the top of fruit. Put this top section in a dish, top side up.

**4.** Arrange handfuls of pebbles and crushed charcoal around fruit.

**5.** Add water until pebbles and charcoal are almost covered.

**6.** Place pineapple in a sunny window and keep it watered. In a few weeks, leaves and roots will begin to grow.

**7.** Transplant pineapple plant to flowerpot almost filled with soil mixture. (The recipe for the soil mixture is on page 6.) Put the pot on a saucer and place on a sunny window ledge. Keep the soil moist but not wet.

**8.** Be patient. With proper care, you'll someday have a lush pineapple plant to add to your houseplant collection.

# Apple-Pineapple Surprise

Here's another way to pot a pineapple. This version requires, believe it or not, a sliced apple! Read on.

**You will need:**
- one fresh pineapple
- handful of pebbles or small stones
- flowerpot (8 inches or 20 cm)
- saucer
- potting soil mixture
- water
- large, clear plastic bag (large enough to cover plant)
- twist tie or rubber band
- paring knife
- ripe apple

**1.** Cut leaves from top of the pineapple, as shown on page 46. Slice fruit, leaving 2 to 3 inches (5 to 7 cm) of fruit below. Let top dry out for a couple of days before planting.

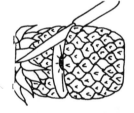

**2.** Sprinkle pebbles or small stones in bottom of pot.

**3.** Fill pot with soil mixture and plant pineapple top so that the exposed part of the fruit is about 1/2 inch (2 cm) under the soil. Place pot on a saucer. Water. (The soil mixture recipe is on page 6.)

**4.** Put entire pot and plant inside a large, clear plastic bag.

**5.** Now comes the fun part! Slice your apple into several wedges and place them on top of the soil, inside the bag.

**6.** Close the bag with a twist tie to seal in moisture.

**7.** After three or four weeks, take plant out of bag and throw away the apple wedges. Keep soil moist. Shoots will begin to grow in about two or three months.

Who needs the apple? You do, if you want your plant to bear pineapple fruit! As the apple wedges ripen inside the bag, they give off a gas. This gas causes the pineapple plant to produce a bud, which will grow into a plant. If this chemical process did not take place, it would take many years for your pineapple plant to produce fruit.

# Pineapple Pine Cone Partners

Maybe your plant will be inspired to grow pineapple fruit if you give it that extra attention explained on page 49. Make some Pineapple Pine Cone Partners to rest among your plant's leaves. These fellows look a little like miniature pineapples — with eyes.

**You will need:**     pine cones          decorations: pipe cleaners,
scissors               buttons, fabric scraps,
glue                   feathers, old jewelry,
yarn, etc.
your imagination

**1.** Find a nicely shaped pine cone. The cone will become the body and/or head of your "partner."

**2.** Look through the decorations and find some interesting "eyes." Buttons, bottle caps, jewelry pieces, or fabric scraps all make good eyes.

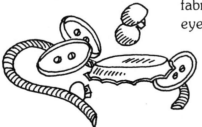

**3.** Glue the eyes on to your pine cone and work from there.

**4.** Use your imagination. Decorate your "partner" any way you like. Don't forget to consider hair, hats, bow ties, ears, eyelashes, etc.

**5.** Arms and legs can be made from pipe cleaners.

**6.** When your "partner" is finished, find a spot for it among the strong leaves of your pineapple plant. Add as many partners as you want and give the extras to your friends.

# Pineapple Yogurt Dip Recipe

Here's an easy and delicious way to serve that leftover section of juicy pineapple. Dip pieces of pineapple into any of these three yogurt mixtures for a tasty, low calorie treat. Come on, try them.

**You will need:**
toothpicks
sharp knife
cutting board
tablespoon
three small bowls
plate
large water pitcher

**Ingredients:**

1-1/2 cups (375 mL) plain
    yogurt
limeade concentrate
orange juice concentrate
lemonade concentrate
fresh pineapple chunks
fresh lemon, lime, or orange

**1.** Place pineapple on cutting board and, working top to bottom, slice off rough outer skin all around. Find an adult to help or watch you while you do this part.

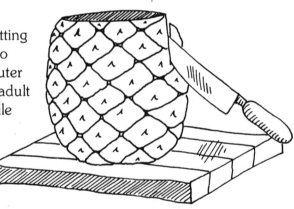

**2.** Cut pineapple in half (the long way) and use knife to cut out tough core. Be careful with the knife. Ask an adult for help, if needed.

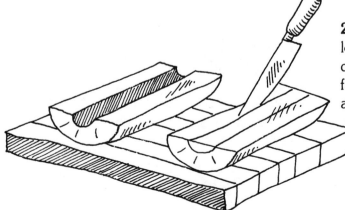

52

**3.** Cut leftover tender fruit into bite-size pieces and put a toothpick into each piece. Arrange on plate.

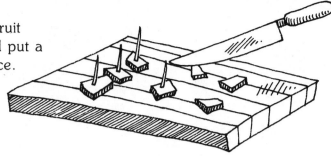

**4.** Measure 1/2 cup (125 mL) yogurt into each of your three small bowls.

**5.** Put 1 tablespoon (15 mL) limeade concentrate into first bowl. Put 1 tablespoon (15 mL) orange juice concentrate into second bowl. Finally, put 1 tablespoon (15 mL) lemonade concentrate into third bowl. Mix all.

**Note:** Add nine cans of water to all the leftover concentrate and make a fruit punch drink. Slice some fresh citrus fruit into the punch and serve it tonight at supper.

**6.** Serve these dips with your pineapple pieces and enjoy all three flavors separately or together.

*Variation:* Try fruited or flavored yogurt with this recipe.

53

# Peanut Plants

**Potted peanuts**
**Homemade "marble" pots**

# Potted Peanuts

Please plant these peanuts in a fancy homemade "marble" pot. Peanuts sprout and grow quickly, so they are a good plant for impatient people. The plants don't last forever, so enjoy them, then save the pot for another peanut. (Note: Roasted peanuts will not grow!)

**You will need:**

a handful of unroasted peanuts in the shell
small flowerpot or "marble" pot
pebbles or small stones

soil mixture
saucer
water
sunny spot

**1.** Place pebbles in the bottom of your flowerpot to cover the hole.

**2.** Almost fill pot with soil mixture.

**3.** Now, remove peanuts from shells. Lay the un-roasted (raw) peanuts on top of the soil mixture. Don't cover them. Just let them rest on top.

**4.** Place flowerpot on saucer. Water soil and place in sunny window.

**5.** Keep soil *moist* but not too wet, and watch for the first sprouts.

**6.** When peanuts have sprouted, plant roots in soil mixture. Space peanut sprouts evenly around the pot. Your peanuts should soon grow into a nice, bushy plant.

**Note:** You can also sprout peanuts in a clear drinking glass using a paper towel, or blotter paper, and cotton (page 30). After they have sprouted, plant them in the soil mixture.

# Homemade 'Marble' Pots

With a little help from adult friends, children of all ages can make these fancy pots. Use your imagination and experiment with a whole collection of colors.

**You will need:**

| | |
|---|---|
| newspaper | water |
| styrofoam cups | plastic spoons |
| spring type clothespin | pencil |
| large plastic bowl or old clean pail | sponge and paint remover |
| two or three colors of enamel paint | |

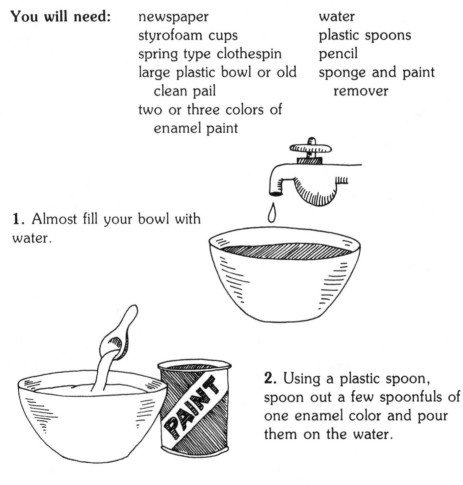

**1.** Almost fill your bowl with water.

**2.** Using a plastic spoon, spoon out a few spoonfuls of one enamel color and pour them on the water.

**3.** Using another spoon, spoon out another spoonful of a different enamel color and drizzle it on the water. You may add a third color, if you wish.

**4.** Now, swirl the paint on the water with a spoon.

**5.** Clip your clothespin to rim of styrofoam cup and, holding clothespin, lower cup into paint and water. Bottom of cup goes into water first. Try not to get any water inside the cup.

**6.** Remove marbled cup and place upside down on newspaper to dry.

**7.** When paint is dry, use pencil to make a hole in the bottom of the cup. Now your pot is ready for soil and a seed.

**Note:** Oops, sorry to mention it, but the sponge and paint remover are for cleanup.

# Avocado Plants and Friends

**Sprouting and potting an avocado**
**Avocado guacamole dip recipe**
**Sweet and cheesy avocado surprise salad**
**Magnificent mango and friends**

# Sprouting and Potting an Avocado

Why spend money on an exotic tropical plant when you can grow one from the seed of an avocado? Sprout and plant the seed. You might try using the nutty tasting avocado fruit in either of the recipes on pages 65-69.

**You will need:**

paring knife
one fresh avocado
drinking glass, small vase,
   or custard cup
four strong, thick
   toothpicks
water

lemon juice
a sunny window

**Later:**

flowerpot
soil mixture
saucer

**1.** With knife, slice the avocado in half the long way. Do this carefully, because you'll have to cut around the seed. Ask an adult for help, if you need it.

**2.** Separate the two halves of fruit and remove the seed. Sprinkle halves of avocado fruit with lemon juice to keep them from turning brown. Wrap fruit and store it in the refrigerator.

**3.** Find a container which is big enough for the avocado seed.

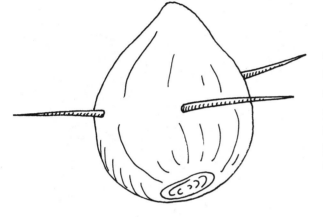

**4.** Stick toothpicks into the sides of the seed. Place them all the way around the seed and about half way up the seed. Ask an adult to help you, especially if the seed is very hard.

**5.** Place the wide end of the seed into the container and rest the toothpicks on the rim of that container. The toothpicks will hold the top of the seed out of the water.

**6.** Add water to your container until bottom half of seed is covered.

**7.** Set container on a window ledge and watch for roots and green sprouts.

**8.** Once your plant is growing well, plant it in a flowerpot almost filled with soil mixture. (The soil recipe is on page 6.) Place pot on a saucer and water the soil.

**9.** Give your plant tender loving care. Then close your eyes and pretend you're in the tropics!

# Avocado Guacamole Dip Recipe

If you're having a party, try serving this special guacamole recipe. It's a tangy Mexican dip for vegetables, potato chips, or corn chips.

**You will need:**
paring knife
cutting board
spoon
fork
mixing bowl
measuring spoons
measuring cup

**Ingredients:**
one fresh avocado
  (ripe)
one tomato
1 teaspoon (5 mL)
  lemon juice
salt and pepper
1/4 cup (60 mL)
  mayonnaise

**Additional items:**
Worcestershire sauce
four green onions
potato or corn chips

**1.** Using spoon, spoon fruity pulp out of skins and into mixing bowl.

**2.** Mash pulp with fork.

**3.** Chop tomato on cutting board.

**4.** Add chopped tomato and 1 teaspoon (5 mL) lemon juice to bowl.

**5.** Now, add 1/4 cup (60 mL) mayonnaise and a shake of salt and pepper.

**6.** Stir until well mixed. (If you like a spicier dip, add 1 teaspoon (5 mL) Worcestershire sauce and four chopped green onions.) Chill.

**7.** Dip in a crispy corn chip and enjoy. Olé!

# Sweet and Cheesy Avocado Surprise Salad

Here's a salad recipe which is pretty enough for company and delicious enough for everyday serving.

**You will need:**

spoon
bowl
waxed paper
paring knife
salad plates

**Ingredients:**

two or four avocado halves
small package fruited cream cheese (Use pineapple, mandarin orange, strawberry, or any cream cheese flavor you like.)
milk
lettuce
lemon juice
any canned or fresh fruit sections or halves
salad dressing

**1.** Soften cream cheese and put in bowl. Stir.

**2.** Add just enough milk so that cheese, when stirred, becomes like whipped cream.

**3.** Peel avocado halves. Be careful with the knife.

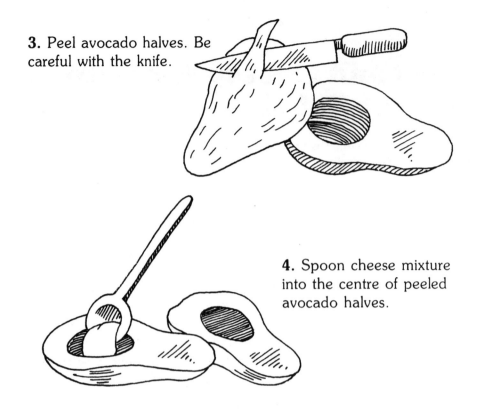

**4.** Spoon cheese mixture into the centre of peeled avocado halves.

**5.** Put halves back together, sprinkle all sides with lemon juice. Spread lemon juice around with your clean fingers.

**6.** Wrap avocado in waxed paper and chill in refrigerator.

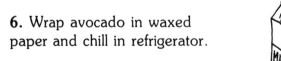

**7.** When avocados are cold, slice into "crossway" slices (not lengthwise).

**8.** Arrange slices among lettuce leaves on salad plates. Decorate with other chilled fruit sections. Drizzle with your favorite salad dressing, if you wish.

DRESSING

**9.** Try this one next time friends or family come to visit. Show them your avocado plant too!

# Magnificent Mango and Friends

Exotic mangos and papayas are usually available, in season, at your local market. Save, sprout, and tend their seeds to produce your very own tropical jungle!

**You will need:**   mango (pomegranate or papaya)  
paring knife  
flowerpot (8 inches or 20 cm)  
handful of pebbles or small stones  
potting soil mixture  
saucer  
water

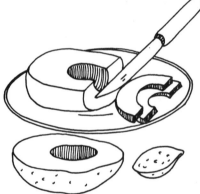

**1.** Cut the mango into slices and serve to your family or friends. Save the seed.

**2.** Prepare the seed for planting by placing several pebbles or small stones in the bottom of flowerpot. Fill pot with soil. (The soil mixture recipe is on page 6.)

**3.** Do not allow seed to dry out. Plant as soon as possible under 2 inches (5 cm) of soil. Place seed in a horizontal position.

**4.** Place pot on a saucer. Water soil and place pot in a sunny window.

**5.** Tend your pot and keep watch. In about two weeks, the seed will sprout. (If you planted a mango seed, your young mango plant will have shiny, burgundy colored leaves. As your plant grows, the leaves will turn green.)

# Popcorn Plants

**Sprouting and potting popping corn**
**Popcorn Parmesan snack**
**Crazy caramel corn**

# Sprouting and Potting Popping Corn

You'd probably rather pop it and eat it than plant it. Right? Plants from popping corn are such fun to grow that it's worth saving a few kernels for both projects.

**You will need:**

bowl
ten unpopped popping
   corn kernels
flowerpot or large
   drinking glass
soil mixture
water
saucer
sunny spot

**Later:**

large 10-inch (25 cm)
   flowerpot or plastic
   garbage pail with hole
   punched in the bottom
saucer or large plate
soil mixture
liquid fertilizer

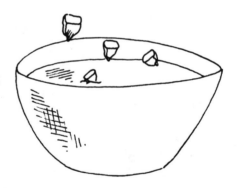

**1.** Put kernels in bowl. Cover with water and soak kernels overnight.

**2.** Remove kernels from bowl. Plant all ten seeds because some of them may not sprout. (You can use the ones which do.) Plant these in soil in a 10-inch (25 cm) pot *or* between blotter and cotton in drinking glass, as on page 30.

74

**3.** Place the pot on a saucer. Tend and water plants in soil until they start to get crowded.

**4.** Pull out all but the strongest plant and let it have all the room. Put pot outside in sunny spot, if you can.

**5.** When your corn plant is 12 inches (30 cm) tall, add some liquid fertilizer to the soil. (Read and follow directions on the fertilizer package.)

**6.** Soon your plant will reach its full height of 5 feet (150 cm). Wow! Save some popcorn for us.

If you sprout your kernels in a drinking glass, watch for this kind of growth:

**a.** In 3 to 5 days, small roots begin to grow.

**b.** Soon after, you will see a sprout growing. It will later become stems and leaves.

**c.** More roots form. Root hair can be seen coming out of the roots near sprout.

**d.** First leaves form. You'll see more roots below.

**e.** Your corn plants are ready to be planted in soil. Transplant the healthiest ones into your 10-inch (25 cm) flowerpot or large pail. Place the pot on a saucer and water the soil.

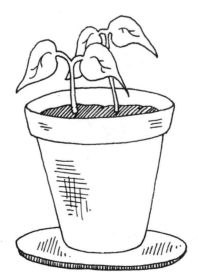

# Popcorn Parmesan Snack

Here's a "Poppin' Popcorn" idea which you might like.

**You will need:**
stove top
bowl
measuring cup
measuring spoons
two large spoons (or
    two clean hands)
small saucepan

**Ingredients:**

popped corn
margarine or butter
grated Parmesan cheese
garlic powder

**1.** Pop popping corn kernels and measure 3 cups (750 mL) of popped corn into bowl.

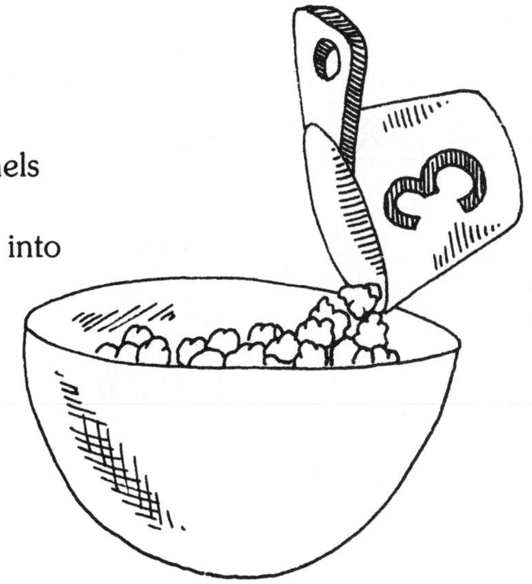

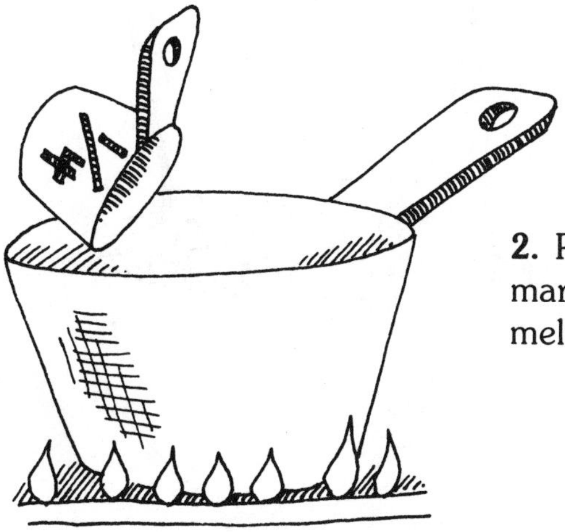

**2.** Place 1/4 cup (60 mL) margarine in saucepan and melt over low heat on stove.

**3.** Drizzle melted margarine over popcorn.

**4.** Sprinkle 1/4 cup (60 mL) Parmesan cheese and 1/8 teaspoon (.5 mL) garlic powder into bowl.

**5.** Toss with spoons or clean hands. Serve to family and friends.

# Crazy Caramel Corn

Add peanuts to this recipe and end up with a wonderful homemade version of a popular store-bought concoction. Great for kids of all ages.

**You will need:**
oven
jelly roll pan or
   cookie sheet
large saucepan
large spoon
waxed paper

**Ingredients:**
8 cups (2 L) popped corn
1 cup (250 mL) packed
   brown sugar
1/2 cup (125 mL) margarine
1/4 cup (60 mL) light corn
   syrup
1/2 teaspoon (2 mL) baking
   soda
1 teaspoon (5 mL) vanilla

**Extra:**
peanuts

**1.** Turn oven to 250°F (120°C).

**2.** Place popped popcorn on jelly roll pan.

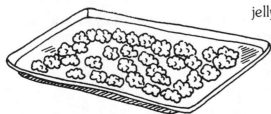

**3.** Put 1 cup (250 mL) brown sugar in saucepan.

**4.** Add 1/2 cup (125 mL) margarine and 1/4 cup (60 mL) light corn syrup. Stir to mix.

**5.** Place saucepan over medium heat and stir until mixture boils. You may want to have an adult help with this part.

**6.** Turn heat to low and simmer mixture for two minutes.

**7.** Remove from heat and stir in 1/2 teaspoon (2 mL) baking soda and 1 teaspoon (5 mL) vanilla.

**8.** Now, drizzle brown sugar mixture over popcorn and mix with spoon.

**9.** Bake popcorn for 30 minutes. Stir twice during baking time.

**10.** Remove popcorn from pan *right away* and cool on waxed paper.

# Special Sprouted Plants to Eat

**Growing plants to eat**
**Banana-peanut butter sproutwich**
**Mustard or cress seeds**
**Sprout-munching salad**

# Growing Plants to Eat

Watch carefully. You won't have much time to enjoy the sight of these new sprouts. In just four or five days, your young plants are ready to eat.

**You will need:**
a clean glass jar
measuring spoons
rubber band
a square of cheesecloth
   or other loose-weave
   fabric (try a J-cloth)

1/4 cup (30 mL) alfalfa
   seeds or mung beans
water
a dark place
a refrigerator

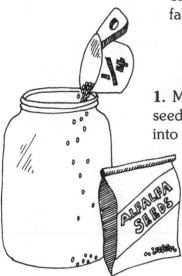

**1.** Measure 1/4 cup (30 mL) seeds or beans and put them into your glass jar.

**2.** Fill the jar with water.

**3.** Cover jar top with cheesecloth or fabric. Use rubber band to hold fabric in place.

**4.** Allow seeds to soak in water overnight.

**5.** In the morning, drain out water through cheesecloth. Rinse seeds with fresh water. Drain again.

**6.** Now the fun! Place the glass jar on its side in a very dark place and let it stay overnight.

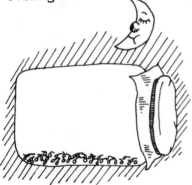

**7.** The next morning, rinse with water and drain again. Do the same later in the afternoon. After each rinsing, return jar to dark place.

**8.** Rinse and drain morning and afternoon until your seeds sprout. Then store them in the refrigerator.

# Banana-Peanut Butter Sproutwich

Your sprouts are ready to eat. Believe it or not, sprouts taste wonderful on sandwiches or in salads. Here's an open-face sprout-peanut butter sandwich recipe which our children love.

**You will need:**
spoon
fork
bowl
paring knife
measuring cup

**Ingredients:**
whole wheat bread
fresh sprouts
one banana
1 cup (250 mL) tofu (if you don't have any tofu, just add more peanut butter)
1/2 cup (125 mL) peanut butter
one lemon

**1.** Mash banana with fork and put in bowl.

**2.** Cut lemon in half and squeeze 1 teaspoon (5 mL) juice into bowl.

**3.** Add 1 cup (250 mL) tofu and 1/2 cup (125 mL) peanut butter. Stir.

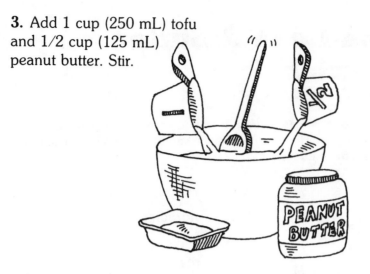

**4.** Spread mixture on whole wheat bread.

**5.** Sprinkle with fresh sprouts.

**6.** Eat your delicious open-face sprout sandwich and smile!

# Mustard or Cress Seeds

Sprout mustard or cress seeds on paper towelling. Then harvest your crop. Your sprouts will be rich in vitamins, tender, and oh so delicious.

**You will need:**    paper toweling
two plates
mustard or cress seeds
water

**1.** Place a few sheets of paper toweling on a plate.

**2.** Moisten the toweling with water. Paper should be *moist* or *damp* but not standing in water.

**3.** Sprinkle seeds on toweling. Make sure the seeds are not on top of each other.

**4.** Now, cover seeds and toweling with another plate. Keep seeds covered for about three days.

**5.** When seeds have sprouted, remove top plate. Add water to keep toweling *moist*, but not too wet.

**6.** Harvest sprout crop when it has grown to about 3 inches (7 cm) tall. Store in refrigerator.

**These seeds and beans can be sprouted easily:**

parsley          rye
mustard          wheat
cress            lentils
radish           mung beans
sunflower seeds (hulled)   alfalfa

# Sprout-Munching Salad

**You will need:**
bowl
measuring cup
measuring spoons
paring knife
hand grater
cutting board

**Ingredients:**

celery
carrots
nuts
sesame seeds
fresh sprouts
French dressing

**1.** Chop 1 cup (250 mL) celery, using your knife and cutting board. Just cut celery into bite-size pieces.

**2.** With hand grater, grate 1 cup (250 mL) carrots.

**3.** Use chopped or whole nuts and measure 1/2 cup (125 mL).

**4.** Combine celery, carrots and nuts in bowl.

**5.** Add 1 tablespoon (15 mL) sesame seeds.

**6.** Finally, add 1 cup (250 mL) fresh sprouts.

**7.** Toss to mix. Drizzle with tangy French dressing and toss again.

# Cherry Tomato Plants

**From glass-jar greenhouse to porch
Hanging basket and potted porch plant**

# From Glass-Jar Greenhouse to Porch

If you've succeeded in growing some of the other plants in our book, you are probably ready for this project. Growing cherry tomatoes from seed to fruit takes time and extra work, but it's worth the effort. Wait until you taste the end results.

**You will need:**

water
large glass jar with lid
chunks of clay or four small
   erasers
soil mixture
long-handled wooden spoon
seed packet of cherry
   tomato seeds
plant mister or clean spray
   bottle

### Later:

a variety of small flowerpots
   or other containers with
   holes in bottoms

saucers or a large plastic or
   metal tray to place under
   pots
soil mixture
pebbles or small stones

### Even Later:

hanging pot (12 inches or
   30 cm) or flowerpot
   (6-10 inches or 15-25 cm)
soil mixture
pebbles or small stones
plant fertilizer
fungicide-insecticide
   (bought at garden store)

**1.** Wash and dry large glass jar. Lay it on its side and arrange clay or erasers under jar so it won't roll.

**2.** Using long spoon, put a layer of about 3/4 inch (.5 cm) soil mixture into jar.

**3.** Spread mixture and moisten it with water. Make the soil *damp* but not too wet.

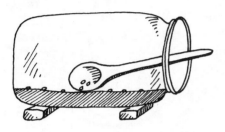

**4.** Pat soil lightly with long spoon. Then carefully sprinkle cherry tomato seeds over the soil. Sprinkle seeds sparingly. Not too many!

**5.** *Mist* the inside of jar with plant mister or water in spray bottle.

**6.** Put jar's cover on loosely and set jar on a window sill where it won't get direct sunlight. Perhaps you can set it behind a sheer curtain.

**7.** Now, watch for the sprouting of seedlings.

**Later:**

**8.** When seedlings are about 2 inches (5 cm) tall, remove the strongest looking plants with your long handled spoon and plant each in a flowerpot.

**Note:** Flowerpots — small pebbles in bottom, soil mixture on top!

**9.** Put a saucer under each flowerpot or use a plastic tray for several pots. Place planted flowerpots in sunny window and water soil when it feels dry.

**10.** Soon you will be the proud "parent" of some strong and husky tomato plants.

**Note:** You will need to transplant your tomato plants one more time, if you want them to bear fruit. Plant them outside in your garden, or try a Hanging Basket or Potted Porch Plant. Just look on the next page for instructions.

# Hanging Basket and Potted Porch Plant

You've sprouted and transplanted your tomato plants. Here are two ways to finish the project. If you have enough healthy plants, why not try both methods?

**1.** Put pebbles or small stones in bottom of a 12-inch (30 cm) hanging pot. Fill almost to top with soil mixture.

**2.** Remove a tomato plant from a small flowerpot (try to keep soil around roots) and transplant it into the centre of a large hanging pot.

**Note:** You can plant *one* large plant in the hanging pot or *two* smaller ones. Leave room around edge of pot for watering.

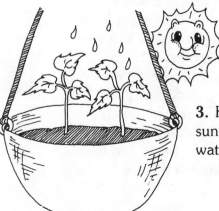

**3.** Hang pot on porch in sunny spot. In hot weather, water soil *every day*.

**4.** After three weeks, *feed* your plant with plant food bought at a hardware or garden store. (Follow directions on package.) Wait three weeks more, and *feed* again.

**5.** Once every two weeks, *dust* growing plant with fungicide-insecticide. (Ask an adult to help you buy this at a garden store.) *Don't dust* after you see fruit starting to form.

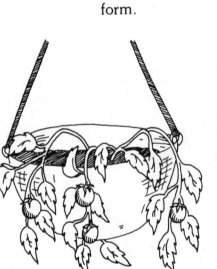

**6.** The tomato plants will grow upward, then bend and hang over the pot. Watch carefully for the first red, juicy tomato. Pick it and enjoy the homegrown flavor.

*or*

Follow the directions for planting cherry tomatoes in a hanging pot, but use a large flowerpot instead. Plant *one* plant in a 6-inch (15 cm) pot. Plant *two* or *three* plants in a 10-inch (25 cm) pot. Set pot and saucer on porch in the sunlight and watch the plants grow. Stake and tie plants later, if needed.

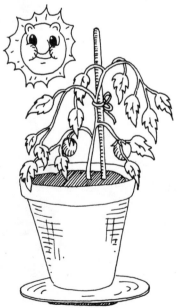

# Apple Plants

**Sprouting and planting an apple tree**
**Apple head puppets**
**Dried apple chips**

# Sprouting and Planting an Apple Tree

You can turn an everyday apple into apple sauce, an apple doll, dried apple chips, or apple pie. If you're really the patient sort, you can also turn that apple into an apple tree. Just remember, it will take fifteen years to produce another apple!

**You will need:**

two or three apples
paring knife
refrigerator
small, covered container
blotting paper or paper
    towels

small flowerpots or recycled
    cardboard egg carton
potting soil mixture
saucers or plastic tray

**1.** Cut apples in half, using the paring knife.

**2.** Carefully remove the seeds. You can eat the apples now, if you like.

**3.** Place the apple seeds in a small container. Cover the container and place it in the refrigerator. Here's where you'll have to be patient, because you must keep the seeds in the refrigerator for six weeks. (This process will make the seeds "think" they have just gone through a long, cold winter.) Record the date on a calendar.

**4.** After six weeks, place the seeds between two pieces of damp blotting paper or paper toweling.

**5.** Keep the paper moist at all times and be patient again. It could take weeks for the seeds to sprout.

**6.** When the seeds finally sprout, prepare the small pots by filling them with soil mixture. You may also use an egg carton for this part of the process. Simply fill the egg carton rounds with soil mixture and proceed. (The soil mixture recipe is on page 6.) Place the small pots or egg carton on saucers or a plastic tray.

**7.** Plant the sprouted seeds about 1 inch (2 cm) deep in the soil. Keep the sprouts moist and in a sunny window.

**8.** When plants begin to outgrow their small pots or the egg carton, transplant them into larger pots. Place these on saucers. Water the soil, fertilize the seedlings occasionally, and give them lots of love.

**9.** Transplant your biggest and strongest "trees" outside during mild weather.

**Note:** It's true that apple seeds are difficult to grow, but it *can* be done, and it's fun to try!

# Apple Head Puppets

Have you seen old-fashioned apple dolls with faces like dried-up prunes? If you have lots of patience, you can make an apple head puppet. Remember, it takes time to generate the wrinkles.

**You will need:**

an apple
paring knife
lemon juice concentrate
bowl
popsicle stick
scrap fabric

wool or fur fabric scraps
small buttons or whole
   cloves (for eyes)
scissors
glue

1. Peel apple, but leave the stem and a circle of peel around the stem.

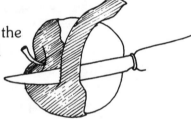

2. Using the paring knife, carefully carve eyes, nose, and mouth into your apple head. (Make the cuts deep, but don't cut clear through the apple.) If you really want to be fancy, sculpt chin, ears, cheeks, etc.

3. Pour lemon juice into a bowl and soak your apple head in it for an hour. (The lemon juice stops the apple from turning a terrible brown color as it dries.)

4. Stick your apple head on a popsicle stick. (The stick will become your puppet's body.) Then tie a string to the apple stem.

**5.** Hang the apple in a warm, dry place. It will take 15 to 30 days for your apple head to dry and shrink, wrinkling like a prune. (Under a 100-watt light bulb, it will take much less time.)

**6.** When the apple is dry, powder the face to give it a flesh tone and spray it with hair spray to "fix" or maintain the color.

**7.** Fortify popsicle stick with glue to make sure head will stay on the stick.

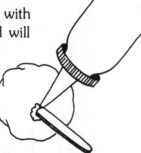

**8.** Decorate body of puppet with scrap fabric. Glue scrap wool or fur to top for hair. Try small buttons or cloves for eyes. Use your imagination and make the puppet look just the way you'd like!

**9.** Work your Apple Head Puppet by grabbing the bottom of the popsicle stick and dancing the puppet up and down from below.

# Dried Apple Chips

Decorate your kitchen or bedroom with a hanging line of apple chips. After seven days, eat your decorations.

**You will need:**

two or three apples
paring knife or peeler
cutting surface

darning needle with large
 hole
string

**1.** Peel the apples and cut out the cores using the small knife. Slice the apples into "chip" size slices, not too thin, or chips will fall apart.

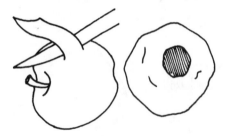

**2.** Thread string through apple slices (one at a time) and thread slices onto string.

**3.** Don't let apple slices touch one another. Use as many strings as you need.

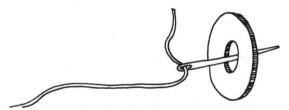

**4.** Hang up your apple slices attaching both ends of the strings to something sturdy.

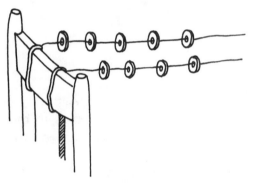

**5.** Hang in an out-of-the-way spot. Turn apples on the string every other day and try to be patient.

**6.** Seven days later, remove dried apples from string and eat. Or, store chips in paper bag until you want them.

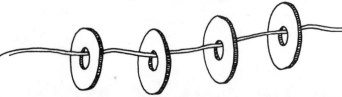